Edited by Cindy Hochman & Megan Merchant

Guest Editors: Cindy Hochman & Megan Merchant
Series Editor: Ami Kaye
Project Manager: Royce Ellen Hamel
Layout, Book & Cover Design: Steven M. Asmussen
Cover Artist: Tracy McQueen

Fonts "National Oldstyle," "Persnickety," and "Metro Thin" designed by
Andrew Leman, courtesy of The H. P. Lovecraft Historical Society, www.cthulhulives.org

Aeolian Harp Series: Anthology of Poetry Folios
Volume 9, First Printing
Copyright © 2023 Glass Lyre Press, LLC
Paperback ISBN: 979-8-9885737-1-5

All rights reserved: Except for the purpose of quoting brief passages for review, no part of this book may be reproduced or transmitted in any form or by any means, electronic or mechanical, including photocopying, recording, or by any information storage and retrieval system, without permission in writing from the publisher.

Glass Lyre Press, LLC
P.O. Box 2693
Glenview, IL 60025

www.GlassLyrePress.com

Foreword

Cindy Hochman, Guest Editor

One of the reasons I'm a rabid fan of anthologies is that each page, and each poem on each page, offers diversity, whether it's in language, tone, or content. It's like opening up a birthday or holiday present, and indeed, poetry is a fine jewel to us devotees of the craft. And we not only get the gift of words, but if a poem is well-crafted, we also get to "meet" the poet as well, since, as we know, there's always a little bit of our own personalities and essences and loves and fears and desires tucked into what we reveal in our poetry.

At the risk of inserting a cliché here, poetry is subjective; that is, what appeals to and delights me, or makes me empathize with the poet, or makes me ponder, or leaves me in awe may not have the same effect on you. Now let me throw in a little anecdote to illustrate this.

When I was a young and budding poet of 21, my friend (another young and budding poet of 21) and I took a poetry workshop given by a more seasoned poet than we were at the time. During one session, we read a few passages from Walt Whitman's 52-stanza "Song of Myself" (of course, we didn't read all 52 stanzas; otherwise, we would all have been very late for dinner that night). I remember as if it were yesterday, and trust me, it wasn't, how giddy I became as I got my first taste of Whitman's expansive observations, sense of social justice, and overall revelry about my own hometown (Manahatta/Brooklyn) and I truly felt as if I were traversing the cobbled streets with Uncle Walt. But, lo and behold, then I caught a glimpse of my friend's crinkled-up nose, and when our instructor asked her what she thought of Whitman, she said, "I don't like him. He sounds like the town crier." *Whoa*, I thought to myself. *Yes, yes, he is the town crier, the Paul Revere of the place where I live but without the dire warnings that the British are coming. That's exactly why these poems speak to me.*

The above story demonstrates the fact that as you pore over the poems in this volume, you will either feel as joyful as I did when I first heard the Old Master who remains my favorite poet after all these years, or you may crinkle up your nose and say "no, thank you" as my friend did, or you may feel something in between. (Hopefully, though, you will find more to get excited about than to turn your nose up at.)

Or, put another way, it is my fervent wish that you find that these carefully selected poems contain multitudes of yawps that remind you why you love poetry so much.

Please read and enjoy this anthology in good health, and may these poetic treasures be balm for your gentle hearts and underneath your boot-soles.

Foreword

Megan Merchant, Guest Editor

When reading submissions, I have found that each poem is a world that I am invited into, allowed to shadow the lines that connect / divide us, understand what is important to the poet based upon where they focus their lens, or carefully arrange words in order to be understood. The poems that were selected for this folio offer these elements and more—these are works that invite a longer stay, a deeper contemplation, or forge a strong connection. They achieve this because they risk "having something at stake," which, if you have taken a poetry workshop, this overused critique might make you cringe, but also—there is a validity to the phrase.

As Kwame Dawes writes in the essay "Vulnerability," "Now, I don't believe that all poetry must expose us in the manner of confessional verse, but I happen to think that a poem's strength must involve some kind of risk, something that makes the poem urgent. And, yes I think that the poem should reveal us in some way."

It takes a lot of bravery to craft a poem with the kind of risk that reveals us, but when created, offers the reader a chance to shift from the role of a witness to that of participant. In this way, a poem becomes a conversation—one flooded with beautiful imagery, a narrative sharing, sweeps of sound, or startling wisdom.

It is my hope that, as the reader, the risks and revelations that are woven into these poems act as invitations for you to linger a few moments longer than you normally would. And when you do, notice what shifts.

...this harp which I wake now for thee
    Was a siren of old who sung under the sea.

— Thomas Moore, "The Origin of the Harp"

Folios

David Cazden	1
Karen L. George	11
N.G. Haiduck	17
Josh Humphrey	25
Michelle Murphy	35
Claire Donohue Roof	43
Russell Sebring	49
Annette M. Sisson	55
Richard Allen Taylor	61
Sharon Tracey	69

David Cazden

Perhaps my personal aesthetic began early, as a teenager, when the iconic Beat poet Gary Snyder came to our house for dinner. My mother was his high school friend in the 1940s and he was the first poet I read seriously, and it was the first poetry reading I ever attended. Since then I've always thought of poetry as being linked to nature, its cycles and forms. I've certainly strayed from this first influence, but always seem to return to the world of owls, rivers, and mountains. Snyder once wrote that the poet faces both the human and non-human world simultaneously and must reconcile the two when writing.

I think that's what I do, perhaps unconsciously, in my own way and voice, informed by my own memories and experience. I've stopped writing for long periods of time in my life, even decades, but always return to it and to this idea—that poetry is the place where memory and nature intersect.

That said, I'm keenly interested and inspired by poets writing today, both young and old. Because poetry is, for me, an evolving art, and I feel it is a continuum, a building of culture, the way a coral reef is built, by many voices, and I'm just happy to try and be a part of this world of words.

Divination At A Hilltop Cemetery

*Frankfort, Kentucky, overlooking the Kentucky River,
near the grave of Major John Bibb, inventor of Bibb lettuce*

I watch vultures trace ellipses
with the compasses of wings,
dropping down a thousand-foot

gorge, above misted water.
Across, a few houses,
smudged dark with smoke

slump into a hillside.
What a place to live,
near a mouth of earth

open in a single vowel,
full of fog and spirits
and so steep and quiet

only a deer could climb down.
Any animal would be at home
in this still place, nibbling

moss off headstones,
ambling to the river
through the scrim of stunted shrubs.

And its hooves, ankles, fur
might glow in the twilight
the way Major Bibb's hands

must have, holding
that first hybridized lettuce—
broad leaves veined

with yellow mist, and its taste
full, like the gorge's depths.
And after chewing that sweet leaf's

flesh, perhaps Major Bibb
understood
the secret of these distances

where the dead linger
and animals wander hungry—
their teeth, hooves and fur

permanently stained
by a mystery in green.

When You Were A Librarian

You traced fingers
over the worn leather covers

of *The History Of The Civil War
(Vol. I)*, then along the railroad tracks

of its spine, gingerly
following broken ties,

chipped rails.
As plumes of engine steam,

musket fire,
gleamed again

in the library darkness,
I wondered if your hands

would melt the glue
that binds all history, page by page,

the way man is bound
—his spine weathered, standing

unread and unspoken. You looked
up, into my skin

where the corpses
of confederate nerves stirred again.

Then you looked down,
returned to your work:

a librarian's task is endless,
stacking books like grain,

sorting and plowing
information in a flickering screen.

And I watched your right hand
graze the keyboard

while your left hand sifted
through the gilt-edged, half-

open pages of your hair.

Midwest Suite

For R.S., 1953-2010

As I drive, each barn, cow,
bridge, and silo

makes a wake of sound.
Prairie grass hums,

sheets of summer wheat
shudder.

Then, settling pools, cisterns,
hay bales, and spools

of baling wire all pass:
unwound from wooden shafts,

the wire gleams like a nerve,
knotted to fences, binding

the wheat in sheaves:
in roadside furrows

they wait, as you must have,
to transform

to dust—to flour and husks—
in harvest light.

On an overpass to Des Moines,
I close the windows and imagine you

buying a tank of helium,
to fill your lungs' balloons

until the string pulled from your hand.
You left without a note,

no words expanding
among peaks and tones

of a landscape,
where each object passing

plucks the air around my car
—as if to exist

is simply to make sound,
to speak, or to be spoken for.

Song To February

As February abandoned its last snows
like fallen linens,

you packed your clothes in plastic bags,
threw them in the hatchback,

slammed the latch and drove.
By noon, ice dripped along the door.

Beneath the lawn, crocus pushed
gloved hands into the snowmelt.

For twenty-eight days, I grew
used to February's

unfaithful breezes,
its sunsets without warmth.

Soon your place
along the couch was gone.

There were no more fearsome storms
rasping through the hollies,

berries crushing red
along the sidewalk,

stained like blood
against the glass.

No more cold and dark
or maps of frost on the windshield

showing where you've gone.
March pushed up

fingernails of flowers,
tossed its shawl of mist

around the tree line's shoulders.
The season ended the way it started—

each surface melting
at the faintest touch.

Karen L. George

I write poems to examine life's dualities and complexities; for example, how moments of joy and beauty are so often intricately woven with an aspect of sadness, regret, or fear. My poems hold a deep connection to the natural world, steeped in a sense of place—gardens, forests, bodies of water, and the wildlife of Northern Kentucky, where I have lived all my life. I ground my poems with concrete sensory detail to fully immerse the reader and create a feeling of intimacy, using language that resonates with rhythm, imagery, layers of meaning, mystery, and an emotional core of compassion, reverence, and longing. I write from a place of unknowing to more deeply understand our connections and disconnections as human beings. I believe poetry can serve as a bridge that joins us to each other and the world in which we live.

Sighting at Mom's Assisted Living

Heading for her lounger, Mom straightens up
from her walker, adjusts her glasses to stare out

the window past the grass patch to the flower bed
where a birdfeeder hangs from a shepherd's hook.

Her voice rises with wonder, *Karen, is that a deer?*
She lost the forward vision in one eye, the other

not far behind. I hurry to her, confirm the fawn slurping.
Point out the squirrel picking through seeds on the ground,

and the tiny goldfinch waiting its turn on the curved hook.
Can you see them? It's hard even for me to gaze

through the screen's crosshatch. Her mouth gapes,
a habit she can't break, though it lets what her lungs

crave escape. Oxygen sluices through tubing,
her arm warm against mine. *Yes,* she says, *I see*

that little dollop of yellow, voice awash
with pleasure. She's not been happy

for so long. I can't bear for the moment
to end. She turns to me, smiles—the child

I never had, never wanted—
the one I can't fathom losing.

Because every moment's an occasion for attention *

As when I open the door of my writing retreat room, a wasp
in the dimly lit hall limps toward me. I almost step on its red-brown

body, mistake it for a knot in the worn oak floor. I lean close,
drawn by its caution-yellow ringed abdomen—a stinger nestled

in its tip. The beginning of December, I expect wasps dead,
or hibernated. It drags its ragged self on long, slender legs.

Male workers die with cold weather, but queens seek a snug site
inside, lapse into diapause until spring, emerge to forge a new colony.

With a piece of paper, I scoop her up, to place where floor joins
wall. I think of Mom, every week more silent, unable to stand

or walk on her own. I don't know that a pandemic will begin
in thirty days, and in four months, she will die. The weightless

wasp tilts away, or did my breath cause the motion?
Its smoke-dark wings are veined like stained-glass windows.

---

* Inspired by, and titled with, a line from Patricia Fargnoli's poem
"The Phenomenology of Garbage"

All Night Long I Dream of Paintings

Massive canvases drift past me, hundreds: portraits,
landscapes, abstracts. I want to purchase three but fail

to narrow the choices. A woman with violet hair floats
in a cobalt sky, stars land in her palms. Mist lifts

from a lake near sunrise, outward-expanding ripples
shimmer. Dizzying swirls of triangles, ribbons, teardrops

of turquoise, fuchsia, chartreuse—a vibrating spiral.
To parchment I apply pigment—a watercolor of rhombus,

trapezoid, ellipse latticed like a writhing school of fish
clustered close. I wake, a knee, hip, shoulder aching,

swim back into the sea of color, shape, pattern, texture.
My mother appears, in her mid-teens, light auburn hair.

Seated at an easel, she paints herself playing a piano,
rendition of when she auditioned for Dad's band. She dabs

silver on the skirt folds of her emerald satin swing dress.
Her fingers curve over ivories arrayed on either side—

the white, open plain of her life.

Your Handwriting

As the anniversary of your death nears,
I feel the pull to see your handwriting, hold

papers you pressed pens against, read
your words, the ways you formed letters

in journals, notes on beloved books,
prayers you wrote.

You braid cursive with printed
letters that slant like calligraphy.

Your *P* in *Peace* plump as a down pillow,
and like Emily, your capitalization never standard.

Your *n* mimics a *u*.
When a word begins with *d*,

as in *dwell*, you form a flat, straight staff
but when at word's end, as in *surround*,

the staff's fat as a baseball bat, and instead of lilting
right, it leans left as if to shield letters beneath it.

Sometimes you break words—
stre tch, kind ness, brea the.

I mouth them, touch their wings and sutures. You
lean near, and I divine the deep murmur of your voice.

N.G. Haiduck

"PUT IT IN WRITING!"

Argument or agreement, words set down in writing have assuredness (right or wrong), authority, accessibility, durability. Putting it in writing is a sure way to capture memory. The wind blowing over the Aeolian harp, like memory, creates beautiful, sad, eerie music, but then wafts, too soon, into the clouds.

Poets say, "This is the way it is for me," and ask "Is it the same for you?" Our stories, based on our common human experiences, are meant to be shared with readers of books and journals or with a circle of friends and relatives. Even stories of tragedy and war are common, and mundane events contain mysteries. The memorable poem tells a common story in a unique voice, just as the wind makes unique sounds against a harp made of glass or wood with strings of wire or grass.

"The memorable poem": the poem we remember for years, maybe memorize. (The poem we want to write.) If we forget our favorite lines, we can read them again. They're accessible, written down. Isn't that why the alphabet was invented? To write down those songs of Homer, those tales of the Trojan War, the adventures of Odysseus. Isn't that why we want to be published? We want our stories to be shared accurately, reliably, now and in the future.

I write poetry to tell my story succinctly in a few lines, not pages. I unravel all those extra words, phrases, sentences to get to the bone of emotion. I read out loud to hear the sound of words, syllables, even the "sound" of the comma or the complete stop. Meter, the heartbeat of a poem, like the bass in a jazz trio, helps to keep my poem from flying off track. Of course, flying off is okay. As jazz players say, "Take it out, as long as you can take it back in." Crescendos and decrescendos, like the rhythm of the wind on the harp, add excitement, surprise.

I put it in writing. This is the way it is for me. Is it the same for you?

Coming Home

My high forehead means I'm smart.
Two lines between my eyes are hereditary.
Every one of my cousins and I have buckteeth,
flat brown hair, and we're all skinny.
We drink Cokes, can all do cartwheels.
Oh, not anymore.

My big brown eyes, oh—let's face it—
my big bosom attracted all the boys.
You could set me down on Water Street
in that little town and everybody would know.
"You're Ruth Marie's daughter."

My uncle told me the whole story:
the tracks along the Ohio,
the rooms above the bakery,
the handsome boy across the hall,
and nobody else home.
Dirty little white-steepled clapboard town.

How his sister, the homecoming queen, cried,
"Oh, Jimmy, I'm pregnant." He covered her
with his jacket and they went to the dance.
She still says, "Nobody but my mother knew."
Everybody knew. Just look at my face.

Legacy

When my uncle says I look like Aggie,
my grandmother, who had straight brown hair
that never turned gray, like mine, I see it.

When my uncle rues how Aggie laughed
at his sister, 17, nine months pregnant
and tired from picking beans and pulling beets
out of the earth, laughed, gave her a spade
and sent her to dig up potatoes, I taste it.

When my uncle recalls how Aggie summoned
them from her straight-back chair by beating
her cane on the hardwood floor in the house
on Water Street, I hear it.

When my uncle swears they hated the man
Aggie married the week I was born
who sold Aggie's things when she died
so his sister had to bid at a public auction
for their mother's brooch, her sewing box,
the porcelain vase their hands were slapped
away from, I feel it.

When my cousin calls to tell me my uncle died
and she's saving his fishing rods, paintbrushes,
tin cans of nails, a dozen hubcaps, telephone books,
toolbox, a cloth bag of marbles, tulip bulbs
in a sack, I smell it.

Hurtling

Child-body pitched head down the basement steps
thumping into the damp gray underground
beside the pile of dirty clothes.
It never hurt too much.

Mother greeted Father,
overcoat at the door, lost job.
"Sissy fell down the basement steps again."
It was an urge like moving bowels or birth.

Barging in or leaving home, breaking things
in one room or another, all balled up,
I knew how to turn over stairs.
It almost brought relief.

Resolutions

I'm never going to learn how to tap dance
or play the piano
I can't change a flat or drive a stick shift
I can't really speak French
tongue throat teeth set to one vocabulary

Burgundy Blaze Suzy Sainte-Anne
too late to invent a pen name
too late to keep my maiden name

I'm the wizened wife
who gives her wizened husband a blow job on blue sheets
the white morning comes
and I feel younger

My muse is blue she is so blue
she is a beautiful blue
her eyes Uranus dolphins
sea and sky and ribbons and flat notes bachelor buttons
sage mountains and moons and moods

Something I was going to do and now I can't remember
treadmill vegetables meditation vitamin C acupuncture
my own amazing power could save me

I'll be optimistic
sit in outdoor cafés on hazy days
go to the movies alone
speak when no one speaks to me

Stop screaming crying pounding the wall when I'm alone
remember the windows are open
and everyone can hear

Josh Humphrey

I started writing poetry in high school, following my first teacher's advice that each poem should be a slice of life. A few decades later, I am still working at it, still finding it unique, still looking for the rare opportunity to communicate myself completely, to attempt to explain the largest things in such small bursts. I am usually grappling with history, the history of New Jersey towns and buildings I have known, the history of my own family. It is ingrained in every word I write and every story I tell. I am sometimes grappling with music, literature, and art, as I try to give voice to artists and their characters. The themes I explore are all human, all universal, all connected to everyday grace. Since I write to better understand the world and, more so, to give some dignity to the world and the people it contains, I work very hard to try to make my poems accessible and understandable. This is the job sometimes of both words and structure, of stanzas, punctuation, line breaks, and even empty space. I hope that a reader of my poetry comes away with some shared knowledge, some empathy passed between us, some foothold as we all reckon with the world as we find it, with being alive. Whether I feel it's one of my few successes or one of my many failed attempts, I am not finished with a poem until I feel like it's true in the sense that it could only have come from me and my experiences. That feels very important in our current time, when artificially intelligent computers can write a halfway decent sonnet. I want my work to be connected to myself and my time here. Hopefully, that, in turn, makes it easy to connect with. This poetry is, above all, my life's work. I thank anyone for taking the time to have a little conversation with me, to share a small slice of life.

River Jumpers

One of my uncles had to go to prison on the weekends
for getting in some kind of fight. They called him
a weekender. They called him a river jumper for a reason
left unexplained. My father would pile us in the Ford
to pick him up on Sunday evenings and he would eat
cereal right from the box with dirty hands, laughing
because it was delicious and it made him think of
his mother's house. We loved my uncle, my brother
and me. He was always a step away from doing something
big-hearted and bad, driving that truck he had that
didn't have a windshield, insisting on taking every cop
who stopped him out to lunch. He gave us our best secrets,
the time he let us sit with him on barstools.
We never asked why my father loved him.
Maybe it was for the same reasons we did.
Maybe it was because he understood about the weekends
stretching sometimes like a sentence, reminding him
that he was not a rich man, wearing those jeans with holes
in the knees, lifting his legs for my mother to vacuum
while he watched football not too loud. He must have
reminded him of that boy who always got him in trouble,
the one who jumped into the Chenango and the whole town
thought he was dead. When the cops came to the door,
he was the one who opened it, a finger marking the page
of a book and hair still wet and Coke bottle glasses missing.
These river jumpers my father knew he couldn't be but
thought about being when he was the last one awake
in the house, maybe the whole block, wearing those slippers
that kept his feet so warm and breathless tight,
those slippers that were probably for his birthday
and that he probably hated as much as the nightshirts
my mother would buy him and the plates she collected that hung
on the walls shiny in the late-night TV light like a hundred eyes.

Rena Stoll on the Titanic

Things They Will Find:
Sixteen dresses which were closer to me
than my husbands, nothing after all
between them and my skin.
My final gift to them—the freedom
of the water, that slow gravity
perfect for dancing without a body.
Three strings of pearls, although
there was only one that mattered,
the perfect old string of my mother.
I return you to your mothers—
flesh within the shells. Hold fast.
One copy of the 1968 *Arlington
Woman's Club Cookbook*,
the well-worn page 62 that contains
my legacy, my recipe for do-si-dos.

Things They Will Not Find:
My first wedding ring, buried like
the man who saw it in a window and
borrowed money from everyone he knew
so that he could place it on my finger
and invent me and make me Rena Stoll.
The Bible I kept around only to hold
the perfect yellow rose I wore in my hair
to my uncle's wedding and he called me
his mountain flower, like James Joyce.
Ten years old, but a woman for a night.
I still remember they lit their dancing
with Christmas lights in August,
and he was so foolishly happy—
I understood for the first time then
that I would actually love a man.
My cats, as they will be fed
by Mrs. Henderson for eternity.

On My Last Day:
I watched a perfect, unexpected sunset.
I ate lamb chops and artichoke hearts for
my grandmother and grandfather, respectively,
and the tiniest, most delicious éclairs.
I played chess with a man who tried to teach me
about baseball. We were both too tired to finish and
so we left the board undone in a room we knew
we wouldn't find again, our moves forever
consigned to the sea, strategies eternally hopeful.

My Words Well Traveled:
I hope I became what they each remembered—
Rena Stoll and Rena Davidson and Rena Stein
and my father's little rhinestone.
And my daughters and my daughters' daughters,
how I love them still in a way so much stronger
than my body, and how lovely their faces,
not yet convinced of it by someone convincing.
I would like to tell them that I am fine, that
you can live in this remembering somehow.
You can live in it forever, just like a tune.

BIOLUMINESCENCE

For my brother Jeff and our other brother television

STAR BLAZERS
We are the Star Force, sent out
to Iscandar after the Earth is
attacked by Gamilon
and flooded with radiation
so that all life will be gone
in exactly one year.
We follow Captain Avatar.
We travel in the Argo.
Our mother works at the
National Community Bank
all summer. Each day we
go in the pool. This is the
last year we will have it.
Afterwards, we sit and watch
television. We sit on top of
towels and slowly dry.
There is no better feeling,
nothing as strangely cool,
our skin remembering the touch
of the water still. We eat
ice pops or Fudgsicles or
the Good Humor Strawberry
Shortcakes. I will never be
as taken care of again.
We are brothers.

BOLDLY GO
I secretly stayed up for you,
until the sound of you bursting
into the house, into the kitchen
to warm up pasta or make a
midnight egg sandwich.
I stayed up for you all those nights
until you trudged upstairs to

the room that still had the wall
of stars and moon you chose,
when I chose the pirate ships and
maps. And then the television
at almost its highest volume,
which was the only way
you could sleep. *Star Trek* by
that time of night, or *The Odd Couple*,
but mostly *Star Trek*. I would turn
on my TV with no sound at all,
and just listen to yours. *These are
the voyages of the Starship Enterprise.
Its five-year mission: to explore
strange new worlds, to seek out
new life, to boldly go …*
I remember when we first came
to Devon Street, it was the first time
we slept apart, down from our
Elm Street bunk beds.
We developed a way to talk at night
by banging on the walls, but
we immediately forgot how to say
anything. We just hit the walls
in crazy patterns. It was fine.
All we ever wanted to say was
"I am here," "I am here too."

INNINGS
Two Thousand was the only year
we liked baseball. The first game of
the Subway Series, you had a party
at your house. It was so long
that the rest left one by one, and it was
just you and me in extra innings.
And our parents were divorced by then
and your marriage was not so great
and we had the jobs that we hated.

I remember it just stretched on,
the unnatural stuck time of that game,
and us on your couch realizing
there was nothing really different
in the winning or the losing. We go on
because we go on together, my brothers.
We go on with the quiet conversation of
our bodies that sustain us, the brilliant light
of these breaths we share from the engines
of our hearts, the bioluminescence.

Degas Paints a Woman with a Towel

In his sixties, Degas did not abandon dancers and jockeys, but as his eyesight deteriorated he seemed to take solace in his pictures of bathers. With little clothing or accessories required, he could focus on the female figure, a preoccupation since his youth.
— Metropolitan Museum of Art gallery label

When my hand touches paper, it traces
a woman, even if I want to paint a house,
even if I am tired. On some mornings
I catch myself drawing on the sheets
before I even open my eyes, always
the same, always the form of a woman.
It is not about wanting to contain it anymore,
not like when I was young. It is not
bragging how I could have built it better.
How could I build anything now—
with tree-stump hands and bellows wheezing?
And my eyes. I used to see clearly and pour
the light in until it all became fuzzy with it
and wrapped in it and beautiful. Now
I just paint what I see. Look at it.
Look at the way it curves—too much here,
not enough there. And yet it is perfect.
Breathtaking. I am the blind man
turning his face toward the sun, opening it
wide to feel the warmth. I am in
the hand of God, tracing the lines there.
Over and over again, this is what I have found.

Michelle Murphy

The first poem I ever memorized was one that my mother would recite to me, "The Owl and the Pussy-Cat," by Edward Lear; the second was "Jabberwocky," by Lewis Carroll (as an assignment in high school). And while the two are both nonsense poems with rhymes and half-rhymes resting on the "edge of sense," it's also the beautiful words coined by the authors, as well as the undeniable visible and invisible musicality that I've always loved.

There's a profile of Anne Carson that Sam Anderson did for *The New York Times Magazine*, and she said this about writing, "We're talking about the struggle to drag a thought over from the mush of the unconscious into some kind of grammar, syntax, human sense; every attempt means starting over with language. Starting over with accuracy. I mean, every thought starts over, so every expression of a thought has to do the same. Every accuracy has to be invented.... I feel I am blundering in concepts too fine for me."

Many of my poetry's beginning images rise out of what's burbling up on the world stage, whether it's the ongoing war between Russia and Ukraine, the drought and fires that have consumed communities across California (and now the flooding), or even the coronavirus lockdown and how it plays out across the planet. There's a strangeness that continues to connect us to our collective humanity even as we persist on destroying ourselves.

As a writer who mostly lives on the sidelines of academia, I'm more or less estranged from the going-ons there. Instead, I read all sorts of things: Wikipedia entries, stunning books of contemporary poetry, wooly essays, food and travel blogs, and then, eventually worn out by thought and personality, sit down at the computer (no longhand for me as my handwriting is atrocious) to see what might surface from the cacophony ricocheting in the unconscious. From memory's suspect confabulations. Which is to say, there is no plan or strategy. Later, after leaving things well-enough alone, I go back in, wearing my excavator hat or my herding hat or possibly carrying my invisible baton in an attempt to create a path to an honest poem.

Sometimes I get there.

After All, Stay Soft

While bombs dust dishes
and shoes, bodies and names
remain inscrutable,
another cautionary
tale gone sideways.

So give them our names.
Who knows one apple
from another?

In the dream,
I am pregnant but
too old to carry language
and so it goes.

Later, in the bar,
there's frenzy
and a quiet corner.
Clocks have been removed,
calendars destroyed.
Motion hones motion.
We eat pancakes in the dark.
Forks hang mid-air,
potatoes and peas
hold the shape of the world.

How to Enough

"Please control the soul's desire for freedom."
Drones in Shanghai over loudspeaker as people sing from the balconies during Covid lockdown

1. Along lush greens
and flower beds,
stones speak.   Listen as they
find your name ajar
but no longer waiting.

2. We jimmy history
into place to make
room for us.
If we have no teeth
to barter   say
our names out loud.

3. Forget this country
of worn wishes.
Stings the scalp and
reckons everything is
nearly lost.

4. All the letters have been

dropped
here and here,   some softened by rain

5. Drink your juice   leave
what is left on the table
next to a hat and empty
briefcase near a typewriter.

Some letters
            but not enough hours
            to make a word.

6. Beached in this
memory that isn't mine
you say we shouldn't talk
for a while   take in the air
then pass over an orange
from your bag.

7. In a century of study,
no one has managed
to reinvent gravity.
Insist, instead, for trees
to speak freely.

Task

I read somewhere
about a monk
who gave names
to honeybees.
She understood
lives were short and
thought they shouldn't
die unknown.

If you think about it,
we almost never hear.
What's being said?

Name the ants parading
past the cat bowl and name a spider
haggling for distance.
This sliding door.
Push sound across a rug.
Phish. Hoo.
Pipes tune in a cross-pollinated elegy.

Ahem.
What is the opposite of this year?
What is crime in ordinary language?

A woman makes a peace symbol
in the snow with the heel of her boot.
Next to it, someone traces a gun.
Scrambling eggs in the kitchen,
we are unaware another war has started.

For the Piano Man Playing on the Side of the Road During the Pandemic

Maybe we'll be okay,
someone will fill the potholes,
repair this frail horizon.
Hearts throw down rock
paper scissors, while another
road's miles dull one into another.

When we kiss this
shuttered world
goodnight,   it's a warbling
                of birds
that spills into our ear
as if reading aloud our names.

And your mother, sudden
& alive again with her laugh,
hangs her hair over
the edge of a blue boat,
skims fingers over water
with what's left of her beauty
while your father,
another piano man,
lugs keys from town
to town on his back,
bewildered by his teeth, &
how in every photograph,
a future of his face
is laid bare,
lank and apparent to anyone
who understands history.

Claire Donohue Roof

My poetry philosophy evolves over time. I believe my poetry is deeply connected to the transcendental ideas about nature, humans, and spirituality. Poetry, for me, is a kind of prayer or meditation. It is connected to where the light falls upon the human experience. Beauty, power, conflict, and evil can all be imagined and discussed through poetry. Life on earth is a fragile but sustaining force. I believe there must be truth-telling in poetry, as the writer experiences this place humans have in the universe. There is one blue-green earth. It is poetry that braids nature and people together. My poetry is also influenced by place and time. I grew up in the Rust Belt of the Midwest. My mother raised us in the city of South Bend, Indiana, but also kept a beautiful garden of fruit, flowers, and vegetables. She taught me the names of trees, and could identify birds by their songs. My four siblings and I were brought up in a house filled with books, art, and music. She was a feminist before her time. She also raised me and my siblings with a strong spiritual faith that, even though rooted in the Catholic faith, had her own ideas about religion and faith. Being the child of my mother, a registered nurse, also gave me an appreciation for her hard work and quick mind. All five of her children, myself included, attained Master's Degrees. We participated in Notre Dame's Upward Bound program when we were in high school. This program integrated low-income urban students in summer classes, tutoring services, and provided much-needed resources to allow students access to colleges more easily. My poetry, I believe, is influenced by that integrated experiences during the 1960s and 1970s Civil Rights and Women's Rights movements. I was taught to use my voice to speak out for justice and to call out injustice. My own moral compass, and my own visions of hope, are interwoven into my work. I continue to expand my creative writing to capture life in its beauty and in its despair.

My ambitions are to balance the world as it is with the body I have—

I want to be a rush of adrenaline—a streak of dark pink azaleas—a fireball in the midnight sky—to go back to Italy and see the flock of birds fly into the blue skies of Assisi. I want to end wars of men with their ridiculously destructive weapons / I want to bring the Alaska snow crabs back in flush numbers. I want to straighten my kneecaps and walk unabashedly towards God. There are places I want to reassemble back to where children can walk home after school without fear / I want harmony in my skin. I want to memorize for weddings, baby births, and funerals / to pray in other languages / I want to let my soul pick out my next career. / There are sequoias, ginkgoes, redwoods, and weeping willow trees I would like to meet / many flowers and poems I aspire to become.

There is jewelry I wish to wear, and then give to my daughters when I am gone / to see my children / celebrate every birth pain that brought them into the world / a broken world / I aspire to have joy / broken and human but undeniable / to be that lyric people memorize / to pass down the good and not the trauma / even if I have already passed down that trauma. / Let me have second and third chances / to talk to angels again, but live on the earth / blue and green as it can be / to talk about death and childhood / I want to hold your hand, yeah. Just like the song / I want to hold your hand.

My Four Children

The children are stars on my body / a shaman shook his head / when I presented my first / my Natalia

He shook his head no to me / told me the girl had taken my magic with her / his smooth

long-tapered fingers preparing me

The second girl does not ever take a breath / takes the breath out of me / leaves diamonds of grief / oh sweet spirit she flies away / my Catherine

third girl arrives in January / slips into the world / as I wander into second epidural / my Rachael

last, a boy, Zachary / larger than my being / erupts from the cesarean as buddha laughs / these are my

journeys into a netherworld of star-studded decisions / break my heartbeats /

wild into my soul/body

The rush of summer daisies my third girl tells me is a first memory / the first / I am tying a string

around her pink, white fist / that I tie to my weathering wrist / so we are not separated

Grand Central Station

my two marriages like rockets explode onto myself, my being, as attempts of

contracts that cannot hold / even water breaks /

these four children live in / out of my body /

they are redemptions / complications / indications

for me to embrace with my love

as they are now in the world / sent from heaven / arrived through my being

through my heart.

Fifth-grade Science Class

Photosynthesis is the green in the trees I pass under as I walk home from school.
The yellow sun in October is glinting through the tree leaves on Dayton Street.

Light, chlorophyll, sugar water, rain, rivers, and oceans all in a cycle of logic and harmony.
I am undone by the perfect circle of late 1960s Midwest world of fire and concrete clashes.

Our backyard is a garden of science and passion, a dreamland of fall flowers and a tire swing.
The sidewalk out front is cracking as the nation is raking up the summers of love and hate.

Yet, fifth-grade science class spoke of order and elements.
Magical incantations of periodic tables and Mr. Spock sang predictable songs into my ears.

It is the year that David will get angry at me and hit me in the face, shattering my glasses.
It is the year our brand-new teacher from college, Mr. Ostrowski, will smoke too many cigarettes.

My mother has us can apricot jam from our backyard tree. There were sour cherries in the spring.
The miniature pear and peach trees bloom, but no fruit. Mom keeps them anyway.

I am the forgetful scientist, reading *A Wrinkle in Time* and Ray Bradbury short stories.
My dreaming self sees fuzzy images of astronauts walking on the moon.

The planets bloom in order on the poster beside my bed.
The galaxy comes to our house in books with pictures of red giants and white dwarf stars.

I speak to angels at night as my father loses another job.
My mother, the red-haired nurse, brings her five children to get our vaccinations.

She wakes me up one day to see two bluebirds mating in the air.
She says this is the miracle.

Will the climate change now tip the world into different science lessons?
Will the science teachers sing like the yellow canaries in the mines?

Pink

Chicago Botanical Gardens Visit 2021 – December 29, 2021

Heat and moisture in winter pandemic,
steals from us visitors our shallow breaths.

The succulent shimmers with wonderment.
The flower dives into the hues of pink.

Pandemic fears close our lungs on outside.
December is ending another year.

But the lush of the pink flower continues.
Sunrays shine through the windows suddenly.

Visitors are falling in love here now.
We take off our winter coats and we breathe.

The pink flowering is showering peace.
In the stillness, pink petals sing our hopes.

Russell Sebring

At its core, my poetry is the result of many years of ongoing study and interest in Buddhism, indigenous spiritual beliefs as expressed in historical text and art forms found around the world, and modern art movements such as Dada, where visual and literary ideology intersect.

In my work, there's an attempt to understand impermanence as life's ultimate reality and free my mind from the confines of desire. For me, nearly every poem is a divine immediacy and an effort to embrace our shared humanity. If one can accept that the universe is infinite, eternally beyond definition and our awareness, then it follows that the devices needed to express oneself poetically are also limitless. Life is poetry. And trying to define the heartbeat of a poem is like trying to capture a moving stream in the palm of one's hand or staring at one's own reflection in a mirror. Both life and poetry are a proximity or juxtaposition. Nevertheless, the poet attempts to grasp the elusive and unspoken, what he or she senses is true, in each their own way. Through my poems, my main objective is to diminish the ego (origin of desire) while I endeavor to challenge the precepts of what free verse poetry can be.

Thus, these tightly structured poems are not meant to be narratives. They're more like verbal landscapes or meditation/word landscapes. The music equivalent might possibly be jazz, but it is actually closer to a type of atonal experimental music. Their interwoven juxtapositions and rigid edifices, inspired by the practice of traditional Japanese haiku, are intentional. There is no clear message to comfort or appease the reader. Punctuation is eliminated to free the mind to make its own connections. When I look out my window, I don't see punctuation. I see the limitations we put on ourselves to make sense of life and to live in peace. Life is not easy. These poems are not meant to be easy. Just as life is filled with beautiful moments, these poems too have beautiful moments that come and go. For me personally, these poems embody faith.

Fall Prey

the last war has been kept to a minimum assembled and thought through as a counterpoint to the urgent impulse texts attached to silhouettes (I need to smell grass earth and the wind from the sea) a strange sketch of maternal envy crippled with aches and pains otherwise happy the afterglow bequeaths permanent concessions whose sole aim is to conceal the frightful term neutrality the sum of stupidity that can never be erased (physically I am tired and calm and feverish) irritable highly sensitive as if on the verge of tears but to survive one must have discrete routines a geometry not an end susceptible in demeanor and the reverse of dignity rage and terror of the present crushed every minute nausea sex clothes come morning an intuition political fights and arguments taxes laundry cleaning friends savings real estate prepare fear scheme protect the future secure your yesterdays the rhythm has become suggestive careful rapid sudden repetitious with various intervals and intensities lairs oscillating beneath black ceilings obey this law of immediacy quiet and shy

Automatic Doors

lists graphs magnitudes autonomous critiques and much counting are the requisite couriers for the preoccupation with repetition the selected material aspects of a precast pedestal the scale of which extends from the continental to the atomic despite the decimated gait an approach so strong that it is difficult to introduce an alternative to its expanse irrelevant or bemused the break comes through acceptance and rejection of the deluge sick with novelty assertions explicata the ambience of identity the soldier cratered by synchronized explosions one standard notch in the heartland obsolete and disinterested its imperium exists as an isolated sound hung flat against a mournful sky the aspiration generates a machine casually stroking the illusion of liberty illusion of presence illusion of the sacrosanct illusion of nature for better or worse profane rituals articulated in godless spaces too tightly bound to their anguish to be anything other than carbon copies of negation no inside no outside the specs located on maps

Thought Feathers

mutilated chance leaps over the abyss unlocking psalms seldom heard in flight a Gothic line seeks the precursor of this new path the limitation and internal organization though an afterthought emerges indistinguishable from the furrowed lips that caress these lavish constellations bent on duration and austerity an imperious composure incarnate wherever apostrophes conclude and passivity begins tactile referents are annulled the contour elapses indistinct zones become essential thereby changing the accident's miracle the specter no longer separable from transfigurations which from gloaming to edict establish the type of tenderness kindled by a persecuted splendor caught in a whirling serpentine maneuver a wasted truth takes its revenge indifferent to coexistence this contrast of luminism and power modeled in chiaroscuro a purely quantitative disaggregation marks the birth dissolving it

Claustrophobia

stack a thousand messages incoherent and lacking in the usual repositories of distraction deem them unconscious myths more convincing than any demonstration of truth cultivate their freedom starve their morals so pretty and right what ease and fascination this cauldron this denial which forgoes providence and yet if cessation ensures a place in the hereafter the exhortations of vandals would still prevail devices begetting leisure begetting symbols an embodiment dependent upon the apotheosis they stir stoned shamans weary legionnaires ubiquitous autocrats proceed according to the promises made bizarre dreams that cannot be substantiated mere minions referential to whim and badgered from corner to corner by a series of environmental concussions resolutely refashioning their complexions in the interests of adaptability the struggle for survival disguises its real appearance awestruck and benign the legend must flatter its patron the unearthly in a rescinded significance removes the burden of sleeping

Annette M. Sisson

From a young age I read rhyming poetry, particularly that of James Whitcomb Riley and Robert Louis Stevenson; I wrote my first poem in third grade. Until my final creative writing class in college, my poems rhymed and adhered to strict meter. I found the move to free verse both liberating and disorienting but committed to eschewing rhyme except for the occasional sonnet and internal rhyme in free-verse poems. I then pursued graduate school in English, specializing in Victorian literature, and have spent my career teaching 19th- and 20th-century British literature. As a result, there is a formal element to my free-verse writing; I am keenly aware of the lines' stresses and prefer to keep them consistent, deviating only for deliberate effect or other poetic considerations. I tend to be careful and charged in my writing, but can occasionally shift into a more spontaneous, conversational tone.

My poems are highly imagistic. In fact, most of my work evokes vivid scenes, places, and moments, typically (but not always) located in the natural world, which often operates as a metaphor for the human world. Through nature I can explore human experiences, feelings, and ideas indirectly while also suggesting that each part of creation—human and nonhuman; plant, animal, planet, cosmos—is intimately connected, an integral part of the whole. My voice emerges through these intersections between our human lives and nature, as well as through experiences, memories, and emotions related to my family and friends.

Finally, I like to think that my poems are musical. I read them aloud as I compose and take seriously how they sound, often spending vast amounts of time playing with words and rhythms. To me, how they sound is also how they mean: the language matters almost more than the poem's idea—very often the language IS the poem's idea. Because I started playing the piano when I was five and have continued to play and sing in choirs throughout my life, the music of the line is hardwired into my brain; it is of the utmost importance to my poetic aesthetic and sensibility.

Our Hands

~ for Nana Barbara

Three months after you died, receded
    into silver haze, a grandchild will be born.

With fingertips that once grazed your cheek,
    I will touch this baby—and he will be yours.

I will cradle him in our hands, picture
    how you would swaddle his body, lose myself

in your strokes. Hunched to my chest, he will drift
    to the sound of your blood sluicing. When he wakes

I will whisper how your gray hair rustles
    on the shoulder of your sky-blue nightgown,

circle him high overhead, a small plane,
    raise him through the veil, arms wide, skimming.

Memo to a Fledgling

Bathe with dust in summer, water in winter.
Preen. Keep your speckled feathers spry—

wingtip and scapula to peel back wind.
Notice, casement glass is not the same

as open air. If wing is damaged, retreat
to a scrap of leggy grass. Flatten your body

in a bed of dirt, picture yourself clay.
Dredge for beetle, termite wedged in crevice.

Choose the slouching sunflower other birds spurn.
Examine each seed before piping it down

the black gullet of your dreams. Let it feed
the skylark in you, silver song like rain.

Unfolding

My daughter hands me
              a fan
                            to disperse the swelter
                                      of Spain
                    black tapered slats
        scarlet roses
                        cuts of lattice below
              the spread of blossoms
accordioned like her life
                      in Madrid
        where she flutters
                              through unlit streets
                scorches her skin
                                under an alien sun
          recites conversation scripts
                                      alone
dances at a discothèque
        while her phone coat   purse   all her money
                    are taken

Still
              she sculpts the hours
                              into alabaster clouds
                      fastens them
                                  to an arch of royal sky

She positions the fan
              between my thumb
                      and index finger
      tilts my wrist
snaps hers open
                demonstrates how to stir
                          the sultry afternoon
                shuffle heat
froth it   like meringue
      how to conjure breath

Woolsthorpe Manor

Here, while the cattle wander off
Newton reads in the orchard, studies
apple descent: *What draws the fruit*

keeps the moon from crashing
into the pasture. Inside his cottage
prisms perch on dressers, tables,

plot waves of sun rays—optics,
fragments of white light. Scrawls
on the walls, now faint: Newton's

physics, germinating, sprouting into tree.
The theory is almost right—his numbers
derived from Euclid's limb. But classical

gardens cannot plot a universe,
trace curves in space, the swoop
of time that slides from its axis.

From Newton's tree Einstein
cleaves a scion that twists into sun's
eye, blind as bombs, bends

into Big Bang. And new grafts
from Einstein's branch divide
into strings, quarks, loops of gravity.

What propagates next? Obsolescence?
Inertia? Love? What to do
but claw across the ice, debate

how much a vessel can bear,
if rock and cloud will pull us under
into winter's icy rush, into drifts—

sleep, the tang of desire, of apple.

Richard Allen Taylor

I dabbled in poetry in my late 20s, decided there was no money in it and (after a brief period of thinking my poems were brilliant, and then finding out they were horrible) decided I was no good at poetry, and quit. In my early 50s my interest in the art revived. I attended some classes, read extensively, and became a regular on the open-mic scene. In my 60s, I retired from my business career and went for an MFA. Why I write is hard to explain. It's hard work, but I'm happy when I'm writing, even when revising. When I go too long without writing, I'm less happy.

Many years ago I heard the poet Susan Ludvigson read her poetry at a writers' conference. Her poems were so powerful and moving, the audience often punctuated the reading with a collective gasp. I remember wanting to write that well—well enough to elicit gasps. My work seldom rises to that level, so often I have to settle for chuckles, raised eyebrows, smirks, snorts, or the occasional tear. My poems tend to be more narrative than lyrical. I like to take ordinary events and situations and elevate them to something memorable or extraordinary. I try to infuse my work with warmth and charm, or whatever mood the subject requires. I am enough of a realist to know that not everyone will like my poems, but I have found a few who do, and it's fulfilling to know that someone somewhere is edified by reading or hearing my work. By "edified" I mean (pick one or all that apply) informed, educated, amused, delighted, surprised, uplifted, or helped in some way.

I was right in believing "there's no money in poetry," but I'm drawn to it nevertheless, as both a writer and a reader. In it I find personal meaning, cultural and historical insights, expanded self-knowledge, and fun. I consider myself lucky to be a writer in a country where, at the moment, being a writer is still allowed.

I Should Have Taken the Day Off

because I cannot walk by your office today
without wanting to come in and ask you
how dark it is on the dark side of the moon,
whether we would bump into mountains
or shade our eyes from the billion bright
lamps of the Milky Way—

but then you would ask
if I saw the latest memo and I would say
no, but I did dream that grass is different
in fields of the heart—softer, greener than envy,
made for tender feet,

to which you will reply
that you received a FedEx package from Atlanta
and I will say that's nice but have you noticed
how blue the ocean is today, the frostiness
of the tall drink I'm holding, the little pink parasol
poking over the rim, the yellow pineapple chunk
floating on top?

Then you will look up inquiringly
from your laptop, your papers, your books, not seeing
the long white beach that stretches forever behind you,
the sand dancing in the wind over your keyboard,
the beat of the Jamaica sun against your bare shoulders,
the wisp of hair fluttering across your eyes.

Tuesday

is grossly underrated, glad to be here, eager to get going.
Unlike Monday, it doesn't care that the weekend is over

or that it was not designated a national holiday.
Tuesday is morning news and handy tool, the good dog

that comes when you call, the horse saddled
and ready to ride. It's different from Wednesday,

which wants to be Friday, or Thursday, already dreaming
about the weekend. It's the second pot of coffee,

fresher than the first, the ball already rolling. It's not at all
like Friday, watching the clock, making dinner reservations.

Tuesday is about direction, not destination, about dreams,
not history, about going somewhere, not arriving. You seldom

find Tuesday hanging out in bars, unless it's on a business trip
and has nothing better to do. If it stays out late, it knows

Wednesday will complain. Tuesday is a go-getter,
the kind of day everyone wants on their team. It almost never

gets invited to weddings or parties (except Mardi Gras) but more
than its share of funerals and insurance seminars. Tuesday works

more but has less time off than almost any other day. Even when
it goes on vacation, it has to tag along with Saturday

and Sunday and the rest of the family, who have already planned
the trip and scheduled the activities, usually without asking for

Tuesday's opinion. Tuesday is alarms ringing, whistles blowing,
the fire engine leaving the station, not the most popular

day of the week, but the kind you might pick
as a business partner, the day most likely to succeed.

What I'm Doing with My One Wild and Precious Life

after Mary Oliver

Since you asked, Mary, I'm sitting in traffic
    nowhere near the swan or the grasshopper
        waiting for the light to change, cold December rain

splattering the windshield, wipers beating like the heart
    of the doe that comes to you in the forest, eyelashes
        flickering over a tender leaf, and yes,

my life is wild, like yours, if the breathless excitement
    of my idling in a gray Honda Accord EX
        with leather seats and 2.4-liter engine

can be compared to your lying in tall grass
    while contemplating migrating clouds and waiting
        for a gray owl with a valentine-shaped face

to swoop down like darkest death to remind you
    your life is precious. Ah, but you asked me
        what I *plan*

to do with my life, and I have described
    a mere moment. What I plan is
        a thrilling day at the office where

my laptop will open
    its one wing and pull me
        into its black pond where icons

float like lily pads and wait to be nibbled
    by a mouse. My office phone will crouch
        to the side, a silent bear sunning itself

in the blaze of a long fluorescent tube
    until I reach for its one black claw. That
        is what I plan.

And before I go further,
    you should know that I *planned* to be
        a pilot, an astronaut, an admiral,

to learn Spanish, win the lottery, run
    for Congress, but all those fragile parchments
        were rolled up

and put back into their tubes long ago, leaving me
    with the wild and precious idea that tonight, Mary,
        I plan to finish your book.

Remembering Tokyo, 1953

I was a child and had no memory of the war.
Too young to know the word *metaphor*.
I knew the streets, covered with snow,

made me think of meringue on lemon pie.
I remember Mt. Fuji in its white cap,
drifts piled against my father's gray Ford,

the happy-face a passerby drew
on the windshield. Dad rented a house for us
in Setagaya-ku. Surprised to find the inner doors

could not be pushed or pulled, I learned to slide them
to avoid punching holes in the rice-paper panes.
My brother and I shared our red wagon

with Yoshiko and Akiho next door, and played
hopscotch, somehow overcoming the language barrier.
Soon, we established international trade, swapped

chocolate cookies for sweet rice treats, unaware
of the distinction between victor and vanquished.
I remember the kitchen had a wooden icebox

instead of a refrigerator, because, I later learned,
most of Japan's steel had been shot down or sunk.
The iceman came every morning with a new block

in his tongs, an *ohayo gozaimasu* for my mother,
an *arigato* for our business. The tin-can man rolled
a cart door to door collecting empties. My father

considered the cans worthless, refused the man's offer
of a few yen, joined the fellow in an elaborate excess
of polite gesturing, as if the two had reached the finals

of a bowing contest. I still remember my brother's
Christmas toy, a clown banging cymbals when pulled
across the floor. Rough play scraped the clown's top layer

of paint. We found a Havoline Motor Oil can underneath.
Days later, I rolled like a clown across the floor
of a lurching streetcar in Ginza, then jumped up and ran

to my mother, expecting sympathy. She chided me
for my carelessness. At the Imperial Palace grounds,
pretty girls in kimonos posed for Dad's camera

with Tommy and me in our cowboy hats, cherry blossoms
spinning like cotton candy in the background. Later,
our landlady, Mrs. Nikawa-san, gave us candy.

Afterward, Mom caught us banging on her door
like beggars, asking for more. Much later I learned
that "san" could mean either Mr. or Mrs.

which meant we had called her "Mrs. Mrs. Nikawa"
all the months we lived there. Apples were fifty yen
on the street. I can still say *konichiwa* in greeting,

answer the phone *moshi-moshi*, ask my brother
to "pass the butter *dozo*." I remember we walked
the sidewalks without fear. The Emperor had guaranteed

our safety. I don't remember any talk of Hiroshima, but
we were children then. We had no memory of the war.

Sharon Tracey

Nature and art have always been central to my writing life, reflecting both my environmental work over the years and my love of visual art, both as viewer and maker. An image is sometimes the springboard for a poem while the act of noticing and naming feels like a way into closer attention and empathy, a way to frame beauty. As a lifelong student of natural history, I'm also a bit obsessed with field guides—both the Latin nomenclature and the details of a species' life history. I grapple with the human tendency to put ourselves in the center of the universe, with other sentient beings a sideshow to our own experience. I often try to shift the focal point in my poems to give breathing room and agency to other animals and living things, and to spark a path, a way to recognize and bear witness. Coyotes, whales, and bluebirds. Meadows, trees, and forests. Extinction and rebirth. Symbiosis and mutualism. How we live together and depend on one another, or not. Landscape and geography are also powerful forces for me, how particular places shape us. In the midst of all this, the act of writing poetry has become almost a kind of spiritual practice, a way to express gratitude and wonder, to explore connections and tensions, to ask questions, to hold grace, grief, and devotion. I love how poetry can strip things down and, through metaphor, music, color, and form, maybe nudge us closer to empathy, to tenderness, to see more deeply or differently.

Rain Birds and Related Questions

Did you know that mourning doves coo
without opening their beaks,
that cooing is the wooing
male birds do? That wings can whistle?
Did you know that fish talk to one another,
can sound like crickets by clicking teeth
or rubbing fins?
That the ocean is filled with conversation?
Do you ever forget the world
is always ending?
Recently, I read about a flower named
for its own extinction, *Gasteranthus extinctus*,
an orange-petaled beauty rediscovered
on a ridge in Ecuador.
Should this be celebrated or mourned?
Is it evidence of progress or just a fire
not put out, illuminating
the green rain for one more day?

Shape-shifting in Topanga Canyon

—Topanga: where the mountain meets the sea
　　　　　　　　　　　　　The Tongva

Coyote's call cuts the wind
and wakes me, the summer moon full,
the canyon rimmed midnight blue
as if all water and light,
my dream following the path
of the day's news—
the thin white
beluga whale
who swam a southern path
from arctic waters
and found himself in France
along the Seine.
They tried to feed him dead
herring and live trout.
They hoped to save him
as they hoisted high
with heavy nets his body,
more sardine-like than cetacean,
so emaciated. There then
was a shape-shifting
above my bed—
a whale's glow in the echo
of coyote. The beluga's
final thoughts unknown,
as he was spooned
from the silver river—
too fresh, too warm.

The Blues

Blue is not hysterical. Feels historical.
Consistent in the chord it strikes—

Bring Agapanthus. Delphinium. Lobelia.
Mary's blue cloak. A blue evening
even as it recedes.

Bring Borage. The one that mutes
melancholy, becalms. Bring
Bluets, enough to fill an urn.

If I could, I'd call for Bluebirds.

But there is no such thing as a blue bird.
No blue pigment, just a structural color
produced by light interacting with a feather.

We see blue where there is none and for this
I should be glad.

Summer Rental on Ocean Farm Road

We slept in Mr. Pough's bedroom
though we didn't know it then,
the place where he passed away
on a June evening years ago.
Some days are draped in yellow.

The house was set in meadow,
replete with orange butterfly
weed and summer birds
and we could taste the salt
and hear the humid sea.

I walked through the house
searching for clues. And
that's when I found him,
the author of the Audubon
bird guides and a founder

of the Nature Conservancy.
A photograph, telltale books,
a quarter-inch of settled dust.
I've never thought that souls
leave the land they love.

I opened the door and walked
out into the meadow.
I heard the yellow warblers.
I saw the meadowlarks.
I met a man I never knew.

Publication Credits

David Cazden

Passages North—"Divination At A Hilltop Cemetery," "When You Were A Librarian"

Pirene's Fountain—"Song To February"

Karen L. George

"Sighting at Mom's Assisted Living" was originally published in *Blue Heron Review*, April 2022

"Because every moment's an occasion for attention" was originally published in *Slippery Elm* as winner of their 2022 Poetry Contest, November 2022

"All Night Long I Dream of Paintings" was originally published in *Blue Heron Review*, May 2021

"Your Handwriting" was originally published in *94 Creations*, Spring 2014, and by Dos Madres Press in my poetry collection *Swim Your Way Back*, 2014

N.G. Haiduck

Hanging Loose, Issue 96: "Hurtling"

Poetry in Performance (The City College of New York), Issue 38: "Coming Home"

Josh Humphrey

"River Jumpers" and "Rena Stoll on the Titanic" were published in *Paterson Literary Review*

"Bioluminescence" was anthologized in *Rabbit Ears: TV Poems*

"Degas Paints a Woman with a Towel" was published in *Rutherford Red Wheelbarrow*

Richard Allen Taylor

"I Should Have Taken the Day Off"—*Celebrating Life (A Main Street Rag Anthology)*

"Tuesday"—*The Powhatan Review*

"What I'm Doing with My One Wild and Precious Life"—*Iodine Poetry Journal*

"Remembering Tokyo, 1953"—*Running with Water* (Pushcart Prize nomination)

Sharon Tracey

"Rain Birds and Related Questions"—*Crab Creek Review, Spring/Summer 2023*

"Shape-shifting in Topanga Canyon"—*SWWIM Every Day*

"The Blues"—*Silkworm 15*

Contributor Notes

David Cazden has two books of poetry, *Moving Picture* (Wordtech, 2006) and *The Lost Animals* (Sundress Publications, 2013). His poetry has appeared in various places over the years, including *Nimrod International, Crab Creek Review, The Louisville Review, Kestrel, Midwest Quarterly* and more recently in *Anti-Heroin Chic, Valparaiso Poetry Review, The Sunlight Press, Susurrus* and elsewhere. David was the Poetry Editor for the magazine *Miller's Pond* for five years. He lives in Danville, Kentucky.

Karen L. George is author of three poetry collections from Dos Madres Press: *Swim Your Way Back* (2014), *A Map and One Year* (2018), and *Where Wind Tastes Like Pears* (2021). She won *Slippery Elm*'s 2022 Poetry Contest, and her short story collection, *How We Fracture*, which won the Rosemary Daniell Fiction Prize, is forthcoming from Minerva Rising Press in spring 2023. Her poetry appears or is forthcoming in *The Ekphrastic Review, Valparaiso Poetry Review, Willawaw Journal, Cultural Daily, Tipton Poetry Journal,* and *Poet Lore*. Her website is: https://karenlgeorge.blogspot.com/

After living in the Bronx for several decades, **N. G. Haiduck** recently moved to Burlington, Vermont, where she resides with her husband, clarinetist Neal Haiduck. She is the recipient of the BRIO (Bronx Recognizes Its Own) Award from the Bronx Council on the Arts, the Janice Farrell Poetry Prize from the National League of American Pen Women, and the Jerome Lowell DeJur Award in Creative Writing from The City College of New York, where she taught English until 2019. She won First Prize in the Winter Poetry Competition of *Desert Moon Review* and was a finalist for the Ed and Fay Phillips Prize in Poetry, Hannah Kahn Poetry Foundation. Publications include *The Anthology of New England Writers, Cold Lake Anthology 2023, Flying South 2022, Interpoezia Intercultural Magazine, Main Street Rag, Naugatuck Literary Review, New Verse News, Paterson Literary Review,* and *Stories from Home* (A Prairie Home Companion). Her first book, *Cabbie: True Tales about Driving a Cab in New York City, 1972,* is forthcoming (January 2024) from Finishing Line Press.

Josh Humphrey was born and bred in Kearny, New Jersey, but has moved up Bloomfield Avenue a bit to his current town of Caldwell. He continues to spend his days in the Kearny Public Library, however, as its Library Director. His career as a librarian, which is into its second decade, has been the source of much poetry in his life. He has a lovely wife, two children, a dog named Coco, and one hearty survivor of a fish. Recently, his poems have been published in the *Rutherford Red Wheelbarrow, Paterson Literary Review, US1 Worksheets, Innisfree Poetry Journal,* and *Oberon*. He has upcoming work in *Havik* and *Pinhole Poetry*, which will be his first Canadian publication. His poetry has been anthologized in *Rabbit Ears: TV Poems* and *Beyond the Rift: Poets of the Palisades*. His first chapbook of poems, *Afterlife*, which includes the photography of his father, Bill Humphrey, is available through Lulu and Amazon. More of his work can be seen on his recently launched website – www.joshhumphrey.net.

Michelle Murphy lives in Reno, Nevada, close to the Truckee River. Her books include *Jackknife & Light* (Avec Books), which was shortlisted for the National Poetry Series as well as the PEN West Literary Award, and *Synonym for Home* (Wet Cement Press). Poems have appeared in numerous online and print publications, including a portfolio published by *VERSE Magazine* as a finalist for the Tomaž Šalamun Prize. A new book (Wet Cement Press) is forthcoming in the fall of 2023, where she is also an editor.

Claire Donohue Roof is an Assistant Professor of English at Ivy Tech Community College in South Bend, Indiana. She teaches English Composition, Intro to Creative Writing, Intro to Literature, and Rhetoric and Argument. She earned a B.A. in English, with a concentration in Creative Writing from Indiana University at Bloomington, and an M.A. in English Education from Saint Joseph University in West Hartford, Connecticut. She also studied graduate creative writing classes at the University of Houston with the late Ntozake Shange. Professor Claire Donohue Roof has participated in the Writing Resistance Workshops with Larissa Shmailo. She has also worked with the mentor poet Megan Merchant. She has published poems in *Pirene's Fountain, Flint Hills Review, MockingHeart Review, the Common Ground Review,* and the *Deep Water Literary Journal*. She has also published poems in the *Cincinnati Poets Collective*. Her poem "Homesick" won the *Hartford Advocate* Newspaper Poetry Contest. She is the editor of the *Ivy Quill*, a literary and arts journal at Ivy Tech Community College, South Bend.

Russell Sebring is a poet and novelist who grew up near the Manatee

River and historic Gamble Plantation in a mostly agricultural region of Florida known for its orange, tomato, and strawberry crops as well as its scenic white sandy beaches along the Gulf of Mexico. As a boy, he blazed new trails through the nearby swamps and thickets while dreaming of one day setting forth on epic wilderness explorations around the world. By high school, his interests had turned more inward and he became fascinated with the literary achievements and personal lives of his favorite poets, their philosophies, and poetic theory in general. He later graduated with a photography degree from the Art Institute of Fort Lauderdale before going on to work as a journalist, independent copywriter, professional photographer, and web designer. With that chapter of his life fulfilled and after a lifetime immersed in the literary and visual arts, he then turned his attention to composing poetry and novel-length fiction. Russell currently lives near Orlando, Florida, just a few minutes from Walt Disney World and Universal Studios. His novel, *Sparrow Days*, is forthcoming with Curious Curls Publishing in 2023.

Annette Sisson lives in Nashville, TN, with her husband and dogs now that her three children are fully fledged. She is Professor of English at Belmont University specializing in Victorian literature, and in the summer she often teaches study abroad courses in England. She has pursued writing in a serious way since 2018. Her poems can be found in *Valparaiso Poetry Review*, *Birmingham Poetry Review*, *Rust and Moth*, *The Citron Review*, *The Lascaux Review*, *Cider Press Review*, *Glassworks*, *SWIMM*, *SoFloPoJo*, *Typishly*, *One*, and many others. Her poetry chapbook *A Casting Off* was published by Finishing Line Press (6/19), and her full-length book *Small Fish in High Branches* was published by Glass Lyre Press (5/22); she is currently finishing her second full-length manuscript, *Winter Sharp with Apples,* and will soon quest for a publisher. Her poem "Fog" won The Porch Writers' Collective's poetry prize in 2019, and other poems have placed in various contests, including Frontier New Voices and The Fish Anthology. Several have also been nominated for The Pushcart Prize and Best of the Net. She was a Mark Strand Scholar at the 2021 Sewanee Writers' Conference and a BOAAT Writing Fellow in 2020. http://annettesisson.com

Richard Allen Taylor (Myrtle Beach, SC) is the author of three poetry collections, most recently *Armed and Luminous* (Main Street Rag Publishing Company, 2016). Taylor's poems, articles, and reviews have appeared in *Rattle, Comstock Review, The Pedestal, Iodine Poetry Journal, Wild Goose Poetry Review, Asheville Poetry Review, Litmosphere, Gyroscope Review, MacQueen's Quinterly,* and *South Carolina Review,* among others. A Pushcart Prize nominee, Taylor formerly served as review editor for *The Main Street Rag* and co-editor of *Kakalak*. After retiring from his business career, he earned an MFA in Creative Writing from Queens University of Charlotte (North Carolina). In 2016 he and his *Kakalak* co-editors received the Irene Honeycutt Legacy Award from Central Piedmont Community College for service to the writing community. His current project is a manuscript in progress entitled *Letters to Karen Carpenter and Other Poems.*

Sharon Tracey is the author of three poetry collections—*Land Marks* (Shanti Arts, 2022), *Chroma: Five Centuries of Women Artists* (Shanti Arts), and *What I Remember Most is Everything* (All Caps Publishing). Her poetry has appeared in *Crab Creek Review, Terrain.org, Aji, Radar Poetry, SWWIM Every Day, The Ekphrastic Review,* and elsewhere. She previously served as a director of research communications and environmental initiatives at the University of Massachusetts Amherst. She lives and writes in western Massachusetts. Find her work online at sharontracey.com.

Glass Lyre Press

exceptional works to replenish the spirit

Glass Lyre Press is an independent literary publisher interested in technically accomplished, stylistically distinct, and original work. Glass Lyre seeks diverse writers that possess a dynamic aesthetic and an ability to emotionally and intellectually engage a wide audience of readers.

Glass Lyre's vision is to connect the world through language and art. We hope to expand the scope of poetry and short fiction for the general reader through exceptionally well-written books, which evoke emotion, provide insight, and resonate with the human spirit.

Poetry Collections
Poetry Chapbooks
Select Short & Flash Fiction
Anthologies

www.GlassLyrePress.com